Steady State

of

The Infinite

Time, Free will, Randomness, Cause
and effect, Information and order,
Black holes, Big bang

by

David   J   Franks

Steady State

of

The Infinite

David J Franks   2019

notnotdavid38@gmail.com

Nottingham, United Kingdom

First published on Amazon 15 May 2019

Preface

The purpose of this book is to put forward my theory for an explanation of how the universe was formed, how it works, why we're here, what's going to happen to it and what was before it. This theory also introduces my concept of **'The Infinite'** which extends beyond our universe, important because as you will read **everything is connected to everything else**.

I've tried to formulate a general description of all of existence throughout **all of infinity** – our universe and beyond. The aim is to provide a broad framework for everything, **a general theory of everything.** This includes a common sense explanation of how our universe came about, and crucially, incorporating the latest thinking on major related topics, as listed in the subtitle, so you get the WHOLE picture of existence. With many new and profound ideas, this framework should then be able to accommodate the correct details when they are finally discovered, called a 'theory of everything'. Currently the best theories for these details are: -

The 'standard model' – which describes the fundamental particles and forces, such as protons and electrons;

'Quantum mechanics' – which describes how the fundamental particles and forces behave and interact;

'Relativity' – which describes how large objects, such as planets, space, and gravity behave. And also, fast moving objects.

For the most part each works well, but there are gaps in them and they're not compatible with each other.

My approach has been to use what science already knows and just apply common sense and reasoning to formulate a **believable** theory, which I've called – **'Steady State of The Infinite'**

I've also included discussions on some of science's favourite topics as how I see them, so **lots of new ideas** here as-well, and, for the most part everything seems to fit well together into my theory, thus giving **one of the most complete pictures of existence.** My theory also offers an explanation how and why you're here and how you fit into 'The infinite'.

This book contains many of my own new ideas alongside established ideas, so if you follow science, I think you will realise when you see something **new** – I hope you find that **exciting**.

Thrilling ideas for general readers with a passion for science – and top scientists alike, who are fascinated by existence. I use everyday language and there's almost no maths in it.

Contents

1. You can't have something from nothing.

Some prominent scientists say everything is based on nothing by using clever maths. Others say particles pop in and out of existence annihilating each other to disappear. I say, if something appears to appear from nothing there must be something there to start with, such as an all-pervading aether, vacuum energy or quantum foam – **You can't have something from nothing.** This aether may either prevail over all 'the infinite' or just our universe. If the former is true then it means there is no such thing as nothing or completely empty space.

Because matter/energy can neither be created nor destroyed means that – **There has always been something** in one form or another. Including before our universe !

Because you can't get something from nothing –

That which came out of the big bang went in first. - Including all our universe's order, information and energy.

2. 'The infinite' – Space extends indefinitely.

There are no boundaries, and if there were, there would always be the other side. You will always be able to point ahead and keep going. I will call all of space and everything in it **'The Infinite'**

Many theories including string theory use the idea that there are more than three spatial dimensions. There is absolutely no evidence for these extra dimensions. So until somebody proves otherwise I'm going to assume there are only three spatial dimensions for my theory, up and down, left and right, forwards and backwards, i.e. x,y and z.

It's also assumed according to relativity that gravity can bend space, well if empty space is really nothing then you can't bend nothing. In this case it's the gravity bending the things in its surroundings such as measuring rods and everything else, not the space itself.

However, as you will read later, I'm making a case for the existence of an aether which at least pervades throughout all of our universe and most likely the whole of 'the infinite', including the space between universes. So, in the context of space being an aether or containing aether, I'm happy to accept it's possible for gravity to warp this aether and again any objects in it.

So, when I say it's possible to go in a straight line forever it's not exactly straight as it will be bent by gravitational objects but it should be possible to keep the same direction just as a ship can navigate rocks and small islands as long as you know they're there. So, it's with this in mind when I say you can always point ahead and keep going.

Then comes the notion that space is expanding,

again, if space is nothing then nothing can't expand, and if space contains something it's the something that's flying apart and becoming more diluted that gives the appearance of space expanding.

Some also believe that the big bang was the beginning of space and time itself. If space is empty and nothing then you can't create or destroy nothing and if there is something in the space then that can't be the beginning either because you can't have a beginning of stuff. Stuff (matter and energy) can't be created or destroyed, it's always been there. For the purpose of this book I'm on the side of the scientists who believe that time does not exist, so if there's no such thing as time then the big bang also can't be the beginning of time.

Part of the above belief also includes the notion that the beginning of the universe was a singularity, an entity that was infinitely small with an infinitely high density and gravitational field. Well, if a thing exists it must have a finite size, however small, and therefore it cannot have an infinite density.

If the early universe was a 'thing' then it existed in a space, it wasn't the beginning of space. Since the creation of our universe it's been observed to have been expanding, it's the space surrounding the universe that it has been expanding into. That space may have been empty or if it contains something our universe may either be pushing it aside or blending in with it.

Another version of this Big Bang Theory requires that the universe expands forever. That would require there to be nothing anywhere else outside of our universe which is a nonsense. Why would there be just our universe and nothing throughout the rest of infinity? In addition, some say there will be a 'Big Rip' where the universe tears itself apart and particles themselves disintegrate. Disintegrate into what?

Now, if our universe came from a big bang and is expanding it must have a centre and boundary or edge, if it has an age then it has a finite size. That means it's an object – objects exist in a space, they are not the creation of space as most theories suggest. Consequently, it can't be homogeneous or isotropic and so violates the much cherished 'cosmological principal', which assumes the universe is even and the same in all directions, and from any view point, and has no centre. So, my version of the universe might look different from the centre than from the edge. Also, if we are hurtling away from the centre, then the density of matter behind us might be slightly higher than that in front? - another violation. 'The infinite' however is the ultimate symmetry, it must on average be the same all over and has no centre.

3. Matter

If space is infinite it would be too bizarre to think our universe is the only matter in this infinite space.

If it is the only universe and it came out of a big bang, then the big bang would have been the beginning of time. The trouble with this idea is that, as argued in chapter **1**, 'there has always been something' and that 'you can't have something from nothing' would imply that the initial contents of the big bang had always been there waiting indefinitely and just 13.8 billion years ago decided to explode into our universe.

What would have caused it to explode after waiting an infinite amount of time? Bizarre. One way around this would be to suggest that the universe collapses and then goes bang again in an endless cycle. Why would there be just one universe doing this with nothing in the rest of 'the infinite'? Again, too bizarre to believe.

Therefore, I think it's reasonable to assume **all of 'the infinite' contains matter and other universes**. As there are no boundaries, and if it has always been there, it should by now be **evenly** distributed. If not, there would still be a flow of matter across 'the infinite', also bizarre.

So, I think it's reasonable to assume that there is an even distribution of matter throughout 'the infinite'. This implies **there is a fixed average density of matter throughout 'the infinite',** including averaging out all other universes, if any others. It also implies **there is a fixed average gravitational field throughout 'the infinite'.** Again, any imbalance has had plenty of time to even out.

4. Universes

As mentioned above **'that which came out of the big bang went in first'**.

The only thing we currently know that sucks matter in on a large scale is a black hole. In our universe, black holes are currently forming all over the place. There's one at the centre of most galaxy's and one forms every time a large enough star dies and collapses in on itself.

One possibility is that we and everything else will one day end up in a black hole and the universe will be awash with nothing but black holes.

There are two possibilities from here. One popular theory is that the universe could eventually collapse back in on itself and rebound with another big bang in an endless cycle, but I think that's too bizarre to believe. Also, if 'the infinite' contains other universes, this theory would require that all universes are held in place by some kind of aether or force field, otherwise they would collide and disrupt the cyclic process. Again, a bit bizarre, so thumbs down for this idea.

The other possibility is that it will keep expanding at its ever-increasing rate until it meets up with the rest of the matter in 'the infinite' and merges with it, which, because of other expanded universes might be just all black holes. As these black holes wander about in space, they will attract each other, some from our old universe and some from other universes, and merge to form ever bigger black holes.

Clearly, this process can't go on indefinitely – **there must be a maximum size a black hole can grow to, if not all matter in all 'the infinite' would be in giant black holes by now and we wouldn't be here in our universe.**

Black holes can't just keep getting bigger and bigger indefinitely. I think there would come a time when they reach a critical mass, which I'll call **Black Hole Critical Mass,** and when, one day, they swallow just one more tiny black hole, and explode with a **'BIG BANG'** into a **new universe.**

All black holes must eventually merge with each other and then explode, it's the only way the matter in them can be recycled fast enough. This idea could explain why there were so many large black holes in the early universe. When the big bang happened there must have been a lot of black holes still hurtling towards it, so the large black holes in our early universe may not have come from our big bang !

Part of the reason for the explosion may be due to the actual collision, much the same as when otherwise stable particles smash into each other in a collider and then break up into lots of smaller particles.

12

If our universe was formed from a collision between two large enough black holes then our universe won't be exactly spherical or even throughout. This might be observable; can someone please check.

Whichever theory you choose there must be a mechanism for recycling matter. Matter can't endlessly plunge into black holes, neither can universes keep expanding forever, either way, there would be nothing left by now. **Our universe is recycled matter, formed in an ongoing process with no beginning and no end.** I suggest that universe's have always been, and always will be, forming and dispersing throughout the infinite in this way all the time forever.

At the same time my theory also provides a means for recycling order and re-concentrating energy for a new universe. In other words, entropy is decreasing as matter falls back into a black hole.

5. Connectedness and uniformity – all one and the same

If you accept my proposition that there's matter throughout all of 'the infinite' then I suggest it must on average be roughly uniform and similar everywhere and with the same laws applicable to it everywhere. In order for something to be roughly the same everywhere, there would have to be a connection or something in common across 'the infinite', some kind of aether, vacuum energy, dark energy or quantum foam for example. This, in turn, would imply there is **no such thing as nothing or completely empty space – the whole of 'the infinite' must be filled with something.**

It would be strange if there were an infinite number of ways matter and reality could manifest themselves in, with all 'the infinite' being totally different from one region to the next. So, however many different realities and natures construction kits there are that enables some matter to be present, and the laws that govern it, it can't be an infinite amount, and will thus keep repeating themselves over and over indefinitely from region to region. However many layers or variations there are to reality, it wouldn't make sense for them to apply just in one part of 'the infinite' and nowhere else. **If there's something here there's something everywhere.** Whatever the most fundamental layer of reality is, it must be prevalent over all 'the infinite'. Thus the 'connection' or the 'something in common' throughout 'the infinite'.

Consider the opposite, if the space between matter or universes was totally empty, disconnected and devoid of any fundamental layer of reality it would be implausible to have something in one region with the same reality as in another without a connection or something in common between them. Since, as I argued above, that there is matter everywhere, it would mean all of space would have to consist of an infinite number of different and unrelated forms of matter and realities (bizarre). This, in turn, would need something or a connection, to hold each reality in place and stop them mixing and averaging out, which wouldn't be possible if space was totally empty! This opposite idea doesn't seem plausible, so as I previously concluded, the number of different realities, construction kits and laws of nature can't be infinite, meaning things must on average be similar and connected across 'the infinite'.

Also, if the space between universes is truly empty then there would be nothing for them to cling to, they would be free to move about. Because there is no such thing as 'exact', they couldn't have exactly zero speed, so they would be moving relative to each other (and also spinning). If there was nothing to hold them in place they would be free to mingle and collide with each other, which would be a form of connection. This freedom of universes, and any black holes between them, to move, combined with gravity would mean they are all moving about mingling and colliding with each other. Given the infinite time of existence, this mingling would have made any different universes and realities average out and become similar everywhere.

Again, consider the opposite, if universes were all stationary with respect to each other it would automatically imply some kind of connection between them, such as an aether, in order to hold and maintain this condition. It's not possible to have pockets of matter or universes isolated from each other without something to hold them in place, which again means a connection.

So, **the idea that the space between universes or matter is totally empty, disconnected and devoid of any fundamental layer of reality seems contradictory.**

In the case where each universe is held in place with some kind of aether, itself a connection, and they don't collide there are two possibilities, First, as each universe expands it could merge with a neighbouring universe and mix with new material until the mixture gains enough mass to collapse and cause another big bang. Second, each universe could just collapse back in on itself and cause another big bang with the rebound, and keep repeating indefinitely, along with all the other universes doing the same – a bit bizarre?

Yet another possibility is an aether or vacuum energy throughout 'the infinite' that doesn't have a hold on matter, in which case the universes and black holes could still be free to move about, mingle and collide and therefore connect.

In all cases – **there's a connection or something in common throughout 'the infinite'**.

If everything does mix and mingle it has had an infinite amount of time to do so, it should by now be completely mixed up, with each particle having had enough time to travel an infinite distance (including the matter were made from), this, in turn, would mean 'the infinite' would probably be uniform, and on average, the same throughout!

Either the laws of physics and stuff are the same over all of 'the infinite' or, as string theory has it,10 to the power 500 different types of universes. In either case, the construction kit and laws will still repeat themselves over 'the infinite'. It doesn't make sense that there can be an infinite number of different realities, construction kits and laws. The ones we've got are miraculous enough. It would also go against my idea of a connectedness and uniformity outlined above.

If one accepts there are a finite number of realities, construction kits and laws it must imply there's something in common throughout 'The Infinite' in order to give rise to this situation. All matter must appear alongside or together with something which is common throughout 'The Infinite'. This again leads me to think that there's no such thing as nothing or completely empty space – the whole of 'the infinite' must be filled with an underlying 'something' which is the same everywhere.

The idea of connectedness goes hand in hand with my propositions that there is the same **average density of matter throughout 'the infinite'**, and therefore the same **average gravitational field throughout 'the infinite'**. One consequence of connectedness is that the **average amount of motion, and therefore energy density** must also be the same throughout 'the infinite'. So, it follows that matter and energy must also be in equilibrium throughout 'the infinite'. There may even be a background radiation throughout 'the infinite' similar to the cosmic microwave background radiation in our universe.

As there are no barriers in space, and with an infinite time of existence, any imbalances of the above would by now have evened out.

These average values also mean there is an **upper limit to entropy**. A universe can only keep expanding until its matter density matches that of 'the infinite' - **it can't keep expanding forever**. Therefore, there can't be a total heat death of any universe as some theories predict, some order (information), energy and motion will be preserved. As such there will always be the same **average amount of order or entropy throughout 'the infinite'. There will always be some order** in varying concentrations. If order decayed then by now there would be none left and we wouldn't be here.

Unless the contents of our big bang are totally isolated from the rest of 'the infinite' any theories about our universe must take into account its surroundings. For example, the surrounding gravitational field, and the average matter density of 'the infinite' – which will stop our universe from expanding indefinitely and therefore slow its rate of expansion until it stops altogether.

To summarise, if you accept 'the infinite' is full of matter and that it's similar everywhere then there must be some common aether or substrate to provide a connection that pervades throughout 'the infinite'. **There can be no such thing as nothing or completely empty space. The reason for, or the cause of the existence of "stuff" must be the same throughout 'the infinite'.** This common aether or substrate must be able to interact with matter and would be the reason for matter being similar everywhere and the reason for reality, natures construction kit, and the laws of nature being similar everywhere.

There can't be something everywhere without a connection between everything. If there's some of this aether or substrate in our universe it doesn't seem to have much hold on matter here, so I favour my version in which everything is free to mix and mingle.

Another consequence of this thinking would mean that the aether is an absolute frame of reference for 'the infinite', which goes against relativity? Since 'the infinite' is everything, there is nowhere left for it to go, so on average, it must be stationary by definition.

6. Cause and effect

An effect always follows a cause never the other way around, this is one of science's most basic principles. Every effect, i.e. every event, happening or action, has a cause. This very simple law has several bizarre and profound consequences:

Just as **every effect has its cause**, every cause has its own cause and so on. This line of reasoning should go all the way back to the big bang. It means that everything in the present has a lineage all the way back to the big bang.

Working the other way, it means that for any set of given 'initial conditions' at any particular time, for example, the big bang, each moving particle or assembly of particles will interact with each other, and other things, and cause something to happen – an effect – i.e. cause an effect, and in turn each of these effects will cause another effect, and so on.

This continuous process has led to a specific outcome for our present, that has been completely determined by those 'initial conditions'. All the interactions being governed by the laws of physics. This is a fixed process and it's called **determinism**.

The outcome i.e. the present, will always be determined by those 'initial conditions'. By using the lineage argument above means you can go back as far as you like for those 'initial conditions' – the big bang if you like – or even further – to the matter that went in before the big bang! In fact – **this lineage must go back indefinitely with no ultimate and absolute initial conditions**, meaning – **there's no beginning to everything**.

The only way to escape this cause and effect chain would be to assume that particles or matter has a free will of its own and can change direction or properties on a whim with no reason at all. That would lead to chaos everywhere. Cause and effect also means the future is predetermined, if you take the present as the 'initial conditions' with all its matter, order, motion and energy, all causes here and now, while obeying the laws of physics, will produce effects with a specific determined outcome and so on – **indefinitely** – so – **there's no end to everything** either.

If you know enough about the present conditions then you can predict the future with a limited accuracy, such as forecasting the weather. The future is fixed, if you try to change it, it just means you were already predetermined to try to change it, and that your changed future was the destined one in the first place. Luckily, we have evolved to believe and feel we're in control.

7. Information and order

Continuing with the reasoning above, the black hole that formed our universe was therefore like a **seed** that contained all the order and energy necessary to create the present. In this context – **order can neither be created nor destroyed**. Therefore – **over 'the infinite', there is an average fixed amount of order**, its concentration, however, varies from place to place and with changing and expanding universe's.

As our universe expands it becomes more disordered i.e. its entropy increases (If order can't be destroyed it might be more accurate to describe increasing entropy as order becoming more diluted, so the overall amount of order remains the same but it's just spread out more).

So, it seems reasonable to assume order increases or becomes more concentrated when things get compressed (again) such as when matter falls into a black hole. If universes are indeed formed from black holes this would explain where all the order came from and its **seed** like character. Some scientists believe information (I prefer the word order) is destroyed when matter is sucked into a black hole, I say where did all the order (information?) come from to create the present?

So – **all the order (information?) that came out of the big bang must have gone in to start with.** Our ordered world didn't just come from a random mess – or a clean slate. The order for it first went into the black hole that formed our universe. It looks like **order can't be destroyed or created.**

The contents of this black hole would have been like a giant **seed**, containing all the order necessary to form a feature-packed universe.

Either 'cause and effect' has always been there, thus preserving the order, and applicable to the matter that went into the big bang, and that which came out again, and all the quantum fluctuations with it – or particles had a free will of their own until sometime after the big bang.

If this black hole had crushed all the order out of its matter, then our universe would be uniform and featureless, even the quantum fluctuations had their cause, they were not random. In other words, there can be **no such thing as a clean slate** – just like matter – **order can't be created from no order!**

This black hole couldn't have just been all one homogeneous pure substance, featureless and still, it wouldn't have been able to have any order (information?) and everything now would be featureless.

There must have been a mechanism for order to have been stored in this black hole (and ordinary black holes as-well). It must have consisted of particles or quanta of something so order could have been stored in the arrangement and/or the motion of its constituents – like atoms vibrating in a hot object, and this, in turn, might have given rise to the quantum fluctuations.

Quantum fluctuations are a current way of thinking and are thought to have caused unevenness immediately after the big bang which in turn enabled stars, galaxy's and clusters of galaxies to form – rather than my idea that **the order was already contained in the black hole**.

If my idea of the universe's creation is correct then the final colliding black hole that caused the big bang would have caused a lot of unevenness, ripples or waves and motion, perhaps enough to influence the universe's present form.

However, order will become more dilute as our universe expands but, as suggested earlier – **the universe will stop expanding when its matter density matches that of 'the infinite' so its order, energy and motion will be preserved.**

We are all made from the same elements, chemicals and molecules as each other i.e. the same construction kit, so why are we all different?

Where in nature did the order come from to build something as complicated as my brain?

Part of the reason is due to the rules of interaction atoms use to assemble themselves into ever bigger molecules and in turn the rules of interaction between molecules – the chemistry and biology.

If one looks at the earth, the rocks, the water and air there doesn't appear to be enough order to make a brain. As well as all the ingredients in a unique arrangement and the rules being there, I suggest it must also be important the **order** in which they were brought together and their **energy** and **heat** content, which all, in turn, depends on their **motion** (heat is just vibrating atoms or molecules).

So, a lot of the order needed to make something must be encoded in the motion of the initial ingredients, including the heat motion of the atoms and molecules, as well as the arrangement of the ingredients.

Also, some of the order comes from the arrangement, content and energy of the environment that contains the ingredients. Despite being all made from the same elements, chemicals and molecules as each other i.e. the same construction kit, we are all different not only due to the exact arrangement of them but because of the different motion with which they all came together.

The environment, and any motion it has, something is formed in, also matters, but because this is itself a construction, its form, in turn, depended on the motion, content and arrangement of its initial ingredients.

The environment, of course, is an ever-changing ongoing process. Therefore, for something to form 4 things are needed – an arrangement of ingredients – motion of the ingredients, including the motion from heat – the rules of interaction of the ingredients – and an environment for them to form in. Since there's no exact initial point at which something begins to form then ultimately the order comes from all of the environment and has always been there at any point in time.

Given some motion, the right environment and just the right amount of heat and light – **matter assembles itself into ever increasing complexity until life arises**.

Also, the finished formation and its behaviour are not just described by the content and arrangement of its constituents, but also by its motion and the motion of its constituents – important for describing living things or machines. For example, the same brain would have different thoughts depending on which direction the electrons in it were going.

I would like to suggest all the order contained in a thing, a system, the universe and 'the infinite' is encoded not only in the content and arrangement of its constituents but also in their motion and energy content.

My own definition of information is – **'information is that which represents',** and must, therefore, be created by a person, animal or machine. It is not something that occurs naturally. Things contain order, not information, information is created when someone or something tries to represent the thing or some aspect of it.

Scientists tend to think of things or systems as containing information, I feel it's more accurate to call it order. Reality is made of constituents in a certain order, it doesn't contain information. Information is created when a mind or machine observes reality and forms a 'representation' of it, this can then be re-represented in another form, such as writing, and passed on to another mind or machine. The writing is one of many forms of information.

Scientists also speak of DNA as containing information. I still see it for what it is, a long molecule that is highly ordered, it contains a lot of order – not information. When it duplicates it makes a copy of itself with a template mechanism, crudely put, it's a bit like a machine stamping parts out. In both cases it's the 'order' of the original being passed on – not information.

Order occurs naturally, but information is initially a construction of a mind or machine. Order changes to another order and gets diluted as the universe expands but can't be destroyed, information, however, can be, just set fire to your writing. **Order must always have been conserved, otherwise, there wouldn't be any left now.**

Information informs, if there were no minds to inform there would be no such thing as information. However, order exists whether or not minds do.

There are, infinity to the power 4 states, a moving particle can be in:

1, it can be in any one of an infinite number of locations (even in a finite space);

2, it can be moving in any one of an infinite number of different directions;

3, it can have any one of an infinite number of different speeds between zero and the speed of light;

4, it can also be rotating at any speed.

So, for just one particle, there are, infinity x infinity x infinity x infinity, different states it can be in. For two particles there are infinity to the power 8 states, and for n particles, infinity to the power 4n states.

Therefore, it would need infinity to the power 4n amount of information to describe exactly any system or object consisting of n particles. Does this mean that some system could hold an infinite amount of information? Possibly, but quantum mechanics and uncertainty would prevent one from accessing it beyond a certain resolution. What it does mean is that **all possible combinations of matter can't exist, even throughout 'the infinite'**. Infinity to the power 4n won't fit into infinity!

It's often suggested by scientists that given an infinite amount of time and an infinite number of other universes that anything that's possible will happen and happen an infinite number of times. The common examples quoted are;

That there are an infinite number of other selves all doing something different in other universes;

If you keep putting enough monkeys in front of a typewriter for an infinite amount of time then one of them by chance will produce the complete works of Shakespeare;

Boltzmann brains – It's suggested that Boltzmann brains spontaneously form by chance.

Most complex things either grow, form in a process, or are made. I can't think of anything that spontaneously forms except perhaps molecules.

Given that, as above, infinity to the power 4n won't fit into infinity – **not all possible things that can happen will happen, nor will things that have a moving element to them ever repeat exactly, nor will 2 similar things that have a moving element to them ever become exactly the same as each other.**

(Nor will solid objects be repeated exactly, although they are one of a finite number of different arrangements of atoms, they did not spontaneously form, they were formed in a 'process' involving moving particles. So, to get a repeat of an object you also need an exact repeat of the forming process as well).

The group of all possible happenings is of a larger type of infinity than the type of infinity of 'the infinite' and therefore will not fit in, and so won't happen! Although **'the infinite' contains an infinite number of things and happenings it still can't contain <u>all</u> possibilities.**

'The infinite' is still only playing out one scenario of an infinite number of other possible scenario's – that don't exist, just like the endless, moving patterns a kaleidoscope plays out in only one scenario (but is equally capable of carrying out an infinite number of other scenario's). Why this one and not another? I don't know.

One way to understand this is to imagine two kaleidoscopes turning indefinitely, each one will produce an infinite number of moving patterns and will never repeat the same (moving) one again, and, they will never both make the same moving pattern as each other. Although each one will produce an infinite number of moving patterns, they still won't produce all possibilities, because you can always add another kaleidoscope.

'The infinite' is like a 3D kaleidoscope, churning out moving patterns with no starting point and with no end. As the patterns are moving, they will always be different and never ever be repeated again.

As the infinite has always existed it can't be evolving, so just as a kaleidoscope, the endless and different structures produced in the infinite will always be on average of the same type. Hence my name **'Steady State of The Infinite'.**

8. Randomness

I believe **there's no such thing as random, there's only the unpredictable**.

This is another consequence of cause and effect. If you accept the concept of determinism as explained in chapter 6 it automatically rules out the possibility of anything happening at random because every event, happening or effect must have a cause.

When you see a complicated process and it appears random, it's not random, everything in the process followed cause and effect. The correct way to describe what happened, is, to say that it was unpredictable.

For something to be truly random, the cause and effect chain would have to be broken and particles or matter would need a free will of their own to change direction or properties on a whim with no reason at all. That would lead to chaos everywhere, there would be no order or structure anywhere, and we wouldn't exist.

Because there's no such thing as random the universe and 'the infinite', therefore, work like clockwork.

All the exact order in the world at present arose from an exact order in the big bang – and before. So, the organisation or arrangement of matter (and therefore information?) is not random, and if the movement of matter is considered along with its arrangement there will never be an exact repeat of anything anywhere in 'the infinite' as some scientists suggest.

When you toss a coin, the outcome depends on every minute detail of how you threw it and how it lands, it is not random – just unpredictable.

9. Free will

People who argue for the case for free will cling to a belief that there is a sub-world of quantum particles were the normal rules of cause and effect don't apply and that determinism breaks down. I would like to say that whatever particles or entities the sub world, the fundamental layer of reality, vacuum energy, quantum soup, quantum foam or quantum fluctuations is composed of, still need a cause to change their state or state of motion, they still obey the law of cause and effect. To suggest otherwise would imply they have a will of their own. This sub-level will still be bound by determinism.

So, when you see particles popping in and out of existence from the vacuum energy, it must be because they have interacted with other particles in this vacuum energy, so it's not random whatever the nature of these particles is.

Whether they are particles with specific boundaries or whether they're just fuzzy blobs of energy or strings vibrating as in string theory, they will all be following a set of physical laws, perhaps something similar to Newton's Laws but not necessarily exactly the same laws, and the laws of cause and effect for sure.

If they were much different to Newton's laws, I think you'd be seeing lots of strange things happening.

Also, people quote Heisenberg's uncertainty principal to cloud the issue of free will. This says we can't know where particles are precisely and the momentum exactly both at the same time. I would like to suggest that this doesn't mean to say that they **haven't** got a precise position and momentum, yes, unpredictable, unmeasurable and changeable when observed – but not random.

So, whatever the nature of matter and which laws it's bound by, it's still behaving in a deterministic manner on every scale.

The whole universe and the whole of 'the infinite' are all working in a deterministic manner, to suggest otherwise would mean that particles or entities have a will of their own.

Since matter must always have existed there are no initial conditions. **We're living in an infinitely large deterministic system, with no beginning no end and no initial conditions**. All the ordered and moving components in 'the infinite' are like a 3D kaleidoscope that's always been going with no beginning and will churn out ever-changing patterns forever, and as the patterns are moving, they will always be different and never ever be repeated again. Sorry, when you're gone, you're gone for good (For those who believe there's another you in another universe).

So, all the particles in your brain are going about their business and obeying the laws of cause and effect which means – **you have no free will !** There's no outside entity overlooking to intervene and change your thoughts. All your thoughts and actions have a cause or reason as to why they happened.

If you fancy a peanut butter sandwich, the obvious part of the reason is a signal from your stomach, but why peanut butter? It may be that subconsciously you remember being given them as a child. Your choice had reasons or causes and so was not down to free will, you were destined to eat a peanut butter sandwich.

Arthur Schopenhauer famously said,

"Man can do what he wills but he cannot will what he wills"

10.Time

There's no such thing as time, there is only movement and regular or periodic movement. Such as that in balance wheels, resonating quartz crystals in clocks, swinging pendulums, resonating atoms in atomic clocks and rotating or orbiting planets.

Clocks represent this movement <u>not</u> time. Time is just the name given to our experience of movement and change, one hour is 1/24th of a rotation of the earth it's not a unit or measurement of time, **it's just a number.** It's just easier to say one hour than 1 /24th rotation of the earth. It's easier to say "you've been a long time" than "the earth has rotated a lot before you came".

Clocks just use something that moves in a regular way that is synchronised with the regular rotation of the earth and thus does nothing more than represent the rotational position of the earth relative to the sun. When you ask what time it is, you're really wanting to know how far round the earth has rotated since you got out of bed, or how much more does it have to rotate before lunch.

Clocks do not measure anything, they don't have any sensors or detectors, they're not physically linked to the rotation of the earth or anything else in the universe, they are isolated mechanisms and are synchronised to the rotation of the earth by astronomical observation which can only ever be approximate.

Nowadays clocks are synchronised with time signals from an atomic clock by radio link, but this in turn is an isolated mechanism.

If your clock is synchronised to an atomic clock which is based on the definition of a second then as your clock counts the seconds, hours, days and years it will become slightly out of synchronisation with the rotation of the earth and will have to be corrected by a fraction of a second every few years, this does happen but it's not something most people notice.

General relativity states that time will pass more slowly in a gravitational field, but I prefer to think the gravitational field is slowing the clock, not time. Either way the effect can be measured with atomic clocks, even down to a difference in height of 10 centimetres between two atomic clocks. Your head is ageing slightly faster than your feet. At the end of the day all clocks are only approximately accurate and so must all be synchronised to one internationally agreed upon standard clock.

The most important regular motion to life is the rotation of the earth – days and the orbit of the earth around the sun – years.

Scientists, however, have a more accurate definition for a second using atomic clocks. The electrons that orbit an atom's nucleus can occupy different energy levels and if energised with a maser or laser can be made to oscillate between two energy levels. This oscillation has a very precise frequency and can be used to control a clock.

The current definition of a second is the duration of 9192631770 cycles of radiation created by the repeated transition between two energy levels of the caesium-133 atom (radiation as photons is emitted each time an electron falls from a high energy level to a lower energy level).

Current experimental clocks are expected to be more accurate than plus or minus one second in the life of the universe – better than one second in 13.8 billion years!

Time is only a word used to describe our experiencing of, and observing of, a changing environment and universe. It's is a word used when experiencing the spacing and sequencing of events relative to other known movements or periodic events or to our memory of known movements or periodic events, i.e. our internal sense of movement. It's not real, it's a human thought construct.

Motion ('time') is usually quantised by agreeing on a periodic event or motion and counting or dividing it into units such as seconds.

There's no such thing as the past, present or future, only the smooth, continuous movement and rearrangement of matter and forces.

Using the word moment or now suggests to me 'reality' has been paused and singled out so that it can be called a moment or now. However, 'reality' is in continuous motion, it's smooth down to infinitely small scales, there are no stop gaps, lines or markers and no processes begin or end instantaneously. There is no present moment or now, even an infinitely small one.

The past or future also do not exist.

It's simple, the past was just a different arrangement and movement of the things you see around you now, that previous arrangement doesn't exist any-more – you can't go back to it!

The future doesn't exist because it hasn't happened yet, it's just going to be a rearrangement of the things you see around you now. So, no such thing as time travel.

As for the present, that really doesn't exist either, as mentioned above, 'reality' doesn't pause to create a 'moment'. It's your mind, recording situations and events, that gives rise to your feeling of a 'present'. It takes time, a few tenths of a second, for your mind to take in and process the information from your senses to build a picture of reality, and in this time, things have moved on. You're not seeing 'now' but a slightly delayed recording of past events. Our brains have evolved to subconsciously take account of this, for example when throwing a spear at a moving animal you throw it a bit ahead to compensate. The animal is a bit further ahead than you are seeing, perhaps by tens of centimetres.

The above is about perception but there is an additional physical reason why you're not seeing the present or now. It takes time for the light from an event to reach your eyes, so once again you're only seeing past events. This is a miniscule effect here on earth, but much larger when viewing the heavens. For example, when looking at the moon, you're seeing it as it was about 1.3 seconds ago, the sun as it was about 8 minutes ago and the furthest stars how they were just over 13 billion years ago.

The meaning of 'now' is also further blurred by Einstein's special theory of relativity. This states that it's impossible to say, in absolute terms, that two events separated in space occurred simultaneously. This is because the time interval between two events depends on the speed of the observers, so observers travelling at different speeds and directions will clock different time intervals between the events. One may see it as simultaneous another may see one event happen before the other and yet another may see the events in the opposite order.

I suggest the word time can always be replaced with a reference to some kind of regular or commonly agreed upon movement or sequence of events.

I also believe the word time or symbol 't' can be replaced in science in a similar way.

For example, speed (s) = distance (d) / time (t), becomes d / number of ticks of a clock. So, in science, time will become a number and not a 'dimension'.

If time doesn't exist, where does that leave general relativity? perhaps **gravity slows clocks, not time** (and all other moving things as well). What does Einstein's space-time mean if there's no such thing as time?

11 Miscellaneous thoughts

Why is there a need for an inflation field during the big bang? Why couldn't the early universe have expanded like a hot gas with all its particles bouncing off each other and pushing outwards? If the universe was formed from a black hole the energy for the big bang would have come from the matter having been compressed into the black hole in the first place. There's no need for other explanations.

In addition to the famous question – **"why is there something rather than nothing?"** I would like to add – **"why is the something in motion?"** Because momentum is always conserved it must always have been in motion, and also – **"why does the something have form, structure and order?"** and why this particular order?

My theory has created a need for several new 'constants',

The average matter density throughout 'the infinite'

The average energy density throughout 'the infinite'

An average amount of motion (same as energy?)

The average gravitational field throughout 'the infinite'

A maximum or upper limit to entropy throughout 'the infinite'

Black hole critical mass (before it explodes into a universe)

A fixed average amount of order throughout 'the infinite'

And, if any, an average microwave background radiation of 'the infinite'

The increasing rate of expansion of our universe may be caused by the pull from the gravitational field of the matter in 'the infinite' surrounding our universe, and not by dark energy. It could be this field stretching our universe until it fits back in with the average matter distribution of 'the infinite' rather than dark energy pushing it outwards. There would also be no need to modify laws of motion or gravity, as some explanations suggest.

I think there is **no such a thing as pure substance**. If the contents of the big bang we're all one homogeneous pure substance it wouldn't have been able to store information, or rather order, so it must have been made up of particles or discrete quanta in order to store the order necessary to form our universe. It's because ordinary matter is made of particles with spaces between them, that it has a finite density. Try imagining a pure substance with no discrete particles, it's difficult, would it have an infinite density? Would it be fluid or solid?

Also, if there were such a thing as a pure, incompressible and irreducible substance there can't be much of it, as some estimates put the initial size of the big bang at roughly a million billion billion times smaller than a single atom and others still only at the size of an atom. When you hit a solid object, you're coming up against a force field, not something solid. **A solid object is 99.99999......% empty space**, there's a vast empty space between an atom's orbiting electrons, with which it uses to bind to other atoms, and its nucleus. Since all the nuclei in the universe once fitted into the big bang there can't be much substance in them either.

So, all in all, you are mostly nothing – just a conglomerate of force fields! However, what existed before the big bang still needed to have a finite size in order to store all the order to form our universe. Some main theories about the big bang require that the initial contents were infinitely small and with infinite density, called the singularity, does anyone really believe that? You'd be hard pushed to explain how and where all the order was stored.

It's often said that we're made from stardust. I think it goes a bit further than that. As well as being composed of almost nothing and with no free will, what little you are made of is infinitely old. This may have travelled an infinite distance across 'the infinite', been in and out of an infinite number of big bangs and universes, and an infinite number of exploding stars. When your gone and the universe finally disperses your remains will once again be spread throughout 'the infinite' and recycled over and over again forever !

I think there is **no such a thing as pure energy** either. Most 'energy' seems to be just a result of moving matter. In the case where light behaves as photons then its energy is still just a result of motion.

When light behaves as a wave then I don't know why it has energy, perhaps its motion of force fields instead. When these force fields hit matter they cause the matter to heat which again is just moving matter (vibrating atoms in this case).

For the most part, though energy is just motion of matter, called kinetic energy. Potential energy is just matter with forces acting on or within it, such as bonds between atoms in a spring, that have the potential to cause motion and therefore kinetic energy. Stored chemical energy is a form of potential energy stored as a force in chemical bonds, and in a reaction, this force causes motion that manifests itself as heat, electricity or light which are all just motion of matter (if you count photons as matter).

Nuclear energy is similar to chemical energy but here the forces storing the potential energy are the nuclear forces binding the nuclei together and in a nuclear reaction internal forces cause the constituent parts to fly apart with great kinetic energy. Such as happens in an atomic bomb or nuclear reactor.

So, if there's no such thing as matter, time or energy what's left? – force fields and moving force fields perhaps.

That just leaves the problem of

what is a force?

This is my first book, so, if you enjoyed it, please help me by leaving some feedback.

Thank you